LinkedIn articles

2016- 2018

James Noble

Articles published between November 6, 2016 - June 22, 2018

I was an adolescent Bernbach fan.

Between the ages of seven and thirteen I had the honor of meeting Bill Bernbach many times. And while there are still marketing legends of the sixties who can tell you firsthand what it was like to work with Mr. Bernbach, I had the privilege to see the whole creative revolution through the eyes of a young man.

My dad, to quote Anchorman, was "kind of a big deal" at Doyle Dane Bernbach. On the first visit to meet Mr. Bernbach, I remember entering the monolith of a building and stepping into an elevator that seemed to climb into forever. I don't remember what floor Doyle Dane Bernbach was on but I do remember with great clarity that when the doors opened to the office, my life changed in an instant.

Before me lay the Willy Wonka Chocolate Factory of businesses. Everything was immaculate white and regal red. This wasn't a bank, or a lawyer's office, it was 2001 a year before the movie 2001 even came out. I could see that the future of office decor no longer would reside in beige.

My dad strolled confidently, greeting co-workers like a varsity ballplayer in a high school hallway. As I passed by each doorway something completely out of the ordinary was happening. Two men in suits were flying paper airplanes and giggling like children. A woman had her own office (her own office!) and was pecking away furiously at her Smith Corona. They all had a set of magic markers that put my fifth grade art class to shame. This wasn't 1967, this was something else. It was pure enthusiasm, excitement and lunacy. Of course now it's all commonplace. But back then it was one big Saturday morning cartoon come to life.

My first encounter with Mr. Bernbach was in a screening room the size of a walk-in closet. The smoke was so thick I barely made out the great man's face. With a dapper suit and genuine smile he bent over and shook my hand. I was taken aback, a grown man had never bent over to shake my hand before. After introductions, silence engulfed the six seat theatre. My dad and Roy Grace weren't nervous but they weren't comfortable either. I could feel this man commanded attention. Like some kind of pin-striped General. The room darkened and on the screen came a short little sixty second movie about the Beetle. The commercial ran over and over. When the lights came back on, silence again. Finally the mandate was presented in very few words and what I can only vaguely remember as this, "Not funny enough. I can't understand the announcer, get someone else. And where's the car? Where's the car?" Mr. Bernbach got up looking pleased, flashed Dad and Roy a smile and looked at me and said, "Nice to meet you," that was it.

That was my last time in the Doyle Dane Bernbach screening room but throughout the years I saw all Dad's rough cuts at home. Why? Because Mr. Bernbach said to my father, "The commercial works but if you really want to see if it's great, ask your boys." Thus began the family ritual from 1967 to around 1972 where the old man would lug home a 16mm projector and premiere his commercials on a tripod pull-up screen. I remember my brother John and I sitting cross-legged on the floor awaiting these little movies as if we were about to see Godzilla take on Mothra. Dad would begin his Benny Hill escapades of threading the film through the projector. He'd walk to the front of the living room smiling and explain to us briefly what we were about to see. Always the showman. The flickering would begin and our family room was suddenly trans-formed into a movie theatre. We would see The Funeral spot. The 1949 Auto Show. The Kremplers. The Eskimo spot. And so many more commercials that are now permanently housed in The Museum of Modern Art.

Without doubt, the greatest lesson I learned from Bill Bernbach was how to outthink the competition and do it so well there would be no other recourse than to sit back and marvel. My example is a rudimentary one but I like to think it's the way he did things back then.

One particular afternoon my brother John (now a gifted producer) and I were furiously building a Hot Wheels super hill off Dad's desk. John had a Tom "Mongoose" McEwen Funny Car and I had the arch nemesis Don "The Snake" Prudhomme vehicle. Our races were always close ties and we counted each win with uncanny accuracy in the endless war of who is superior. Earlier, my dad had left with Roy for a meeting.

In walked Mr. Bernbach.

"Hello Noble Jim and Noble John," he said in his well-tailored suit and distinguished grey hair.

"Hello Mr. Bernbach," we said in unison both feeling pretty cool being on a first name basis with the guy who ran the place.

"What? No Volkswagens?" he wondered with a smile looking at our choice of Hot Wheel models.

He walked over in his elegant way. "May I?" he said taking my car and studying the little thing.

"Race?" he said to John.

What? A grown man in a suit wanted to get on his knees and play cars? John nodded enthusiastically. I sat back and watched. John took his chassis and lined it up at the top of the orange track. Mr. Bernbach went to my dad's desk, picked up a few items and started noodling. For a moment we thought he had forgotten about his pending vehicular demise. A moment later he smiled and walked over to the track with his car. He put it next to John's Mongoose.

"Ready. Set. Go," he said.

The cars flew down the track. Except Mr. Bernbachs' car flew significantly faster. It beat the Mongoose by a hefty margin. We looked at Mr. Bernbach in bewilderment. He smiled, rubbed my brother's head and nodded to me like a friendly grandpa. Then he briskly walked out of the office to apply his genius elsewhere.

We went to examine the cars. The Mongoose was as usual. But my Snake was a different story. On the roofline were two paperclips attached by scotch tape. It had never dawned on us to weigh the cars down for more speed. We stared in wonder, and a lesson was learned that went far beyond the confines of our toys.

Win.

And do it with brains. Grace. A little wit. And always, as a gentlemen.

Even if you have to tip the scales.

The Basics: Three tips for writing copy when stuck.

Copy is not the bastard son of a headline. Many young and mid-level writers believe this as I did for years. Influential body copy is crucial if you want to close the sale. And unless you got lucky and wrote something inspiring very fast (you probably didn't) writing powerful copy requires you first reach that emotional state between "I suck" and "I'm indestructable."

Tip Number One.
Always recycle.
Headlines are a terrible thing to waste. It baffles me when copywriters throw out their headlines once a concept is approved. If you've just written a bunch of headlines you probably have a chunk of your copy already written.
An example. I was working on a high-end athletic swimsuit pitch that never came to be. Here are a few half-baked lines to demonstrate a point.
1. *You see an ocean. We see a playground. - Ocean visual.*
2. *We exist because the earth is seventy-five percent water. - Ocean visual.*
3. *No pain. No one-hundreth of a second gain. - Olympic swim clock visual.*
4. *There is no HOV lane here. - Large olympic pool visual.*
5. *This lane requires a toll, are you ready to pay it? - Swimmer on block visual.*

Say everyone likes line number one. The rest of those headlines can be starter thoughts for copy, can't they? Or possibly an opening sentence or a nice ending with a little wordsmithing? Most headline exercises require a lot of thinking. Wring as much out of your hard work as possible. Suppose next month you get a scuba account? Or a cruise line? *You see an ocean, we see a playground* would be a nice opener for a homepage. Save those lines.

Tip Number Two.
Don't worry about grammar just yet.
Your first draft is for tone, rhythm, experimentation and length. Try one word sentences. Sentences with six commas. Write from the perspective of a baby. Heck, throw in a pun if it's worthy of Oscar Wilde.
Point is, do anything to keep your reader's attention. If your customer is going to bail, it will be right here. Your words and your words alone are going to make the sale. It's key to always remember that nobody wants to read your copy.
So make it great.
Then make it acceptable to Mr. Strunk and Mr. White.

Tip Number Three.
Write in chunks.
It's intimidating to see all that Lorem Ipsum. If your brief requires more elements to add in the copy (and what brief doesn't?) concentrate on them one at a time. If you are working on a car write a few nice sentences about the safety system. Then write a few nice sentences about the guarantee. And so on.
Soon you'll have a little smorgasborg of choices you can edit and edit and edit together in whatever order makes best sense for the communication.
Then go to bed and mull it over. Never hand in a piece of copy without first walking away from it for several hours. Check it again. Make sure it's good enough to make your CD smile because you nailed that sweetest of spots.
Selling something.

And making the audience like you for it.

Helmut Krone, Gary Goldsmith, and Roy Grace.

A colleague once told me working in a great creative department is like being on *The Island of Misfit Toys*.

Everyone has their tics. Their particular weirdness. And a healthy disrespect for normal.
So at what point in history did buttoned-up corporate ad managers start accepting, and often encourage nonconformist and occasionally disruptive behavior?

Many historians will tell you it began at 350 Madison Avenue in New York. The office of Doyle Dane Bernbach. I visited there often as a wide-eyed kid and can tell you first hand it was the birthplace of freedom for the odd, the eccentric, and more succinctly, the uncommon.

As long as you delivered.

For me, three people stood out and signaled in no uncertain terms that regulation, routine, normality, and conventional thinking were going the way of the mimeograph copier.

One night my father, who was a young copywriter at the time, led me down a darkened hall at Doyle Dane Bernbach. Dad whispered in my ear reverently, "The man you are going to meet is a genius. I want to introduce you." At the end of the hallway there was a partially open door. The rest of the office was empty, quiet, and deserted.

We reached the door and it creaked open ominously. The office was sparse. There was a draft table tilted up higher than it seemed it should have been. One solitary standing lamp was illuminating everything. Shadows were everywhere. Sitting on a metal stool was a man hunched over like Victor Frankenstein working on his creature. The man wore a pristine white sleeved shirt rolled up to his elbow in perfection, not a wrinkle. His left hand was moving fast, wielding a big stick I later found out was called a T-square. His right hand was scribbling faster than the left.

Suddenly the hands stopped moving. I could only guess he sensed intruders. He never turned his head until my father spoke.

"Helmut, this is my son. I told him about you and just wanted to say hello."

Mr. Krone turned around slowly and revealed a pleasant face with rounded glasses that softened harsh eyes.

He put out his hand and said formally, "Hello. You are?"

"Jim, sir."

"I am Mr. Krone. It's very nice to meet you. But unfortunately I am very busy," it was an authoritative reply that somehow managed to not come off as rude.

Mr. Krone smiled briefly and turned his back. I took a slight step forward to see what he was crafting and he bent over it like someone protecting their PIN at an ATM. There would be no glimpse of the grand experiment from the author of arguably the greatest ad ever created.

Many years later when I was a floundering 16-year-old high school student who felt he never quite fit in anywhere, my dad thought it prudent that I spend some time with the golden boy of the office. Similar to the Krone meeting, it was late and very few people were in the building. Down at the end of another darkened hall one light was on.

I wasn't nervous this time because I could hear Bad Company's "Can't Get Enough."

Loud.

We entered and the man sitting at the table was doing the same thing with the T-square and cutting cardboard with what looked like a very sharp knife. His hair was longish. He wore jeans and a T-shirt. Gary Goldsmith introduced himself. And even though Mr. Goldsmith was likely in his twenties, he still appeared more like an older kid who would get high with me and my friends in the woods.

When my dad shut the door, the show began. From the very start, Mr. Goldsmith behaved as if he were an eight-year-old boy who had just eaten a full box of Sugar Pops cereal. It was nine o'clock and this guy was excited about his job? Enthused about working late? Something was wrong in this universe.

He first showed me his ad that ran in the last issue of Time magazine and treated it like an original Jackson Pollock. He had a drawer full of ads that never ran and explained why the boss didn't think they were right. He kept his mistakes? Something was very wrong in this universe indeed.

Then Mr. Goldsmith brought out his book. A portfolio so good it landed him the job at Doyle Dane Bernbach. Inside, the ads were smart, funny, and insightful, and even I could grasp the meaning for most of them. For that memorable meeting all I could think was this guy was different. And he was getting paid to utilize an overactive imagination. Something I had been accused of having and not in a good way. Perhaps it was possible to fit in somewhere?

Legendary ad man Roy Grace and my father would often hang around our pool during the summer weekdays in swim trunks lying on chaise lounges. I would see a Smith Corona clicking on Dad's belly. Mr. Grace's canvas was a large TV frame pad and he'd be doodling stick figures. Next to them on the ground were frosted glasses and I can tell you with some certainty it was not lemonade. This went on for years and one day it struck me.

My old man and Mr. Grace had a pretty sweet gig.

On other occasions I'd chauffeur Mr. Grace and my dad home from JFK after their shoots in California. My father was dropped off first and then it was about a forty-five minute drive to Mr. Grace's estate. Our discussions were always about the same three things: you could be anything if you worked hard enough, I-95 was the worst road on the planet, and his new commercial was going to be a disaster.

The last topic was told in great detail with a blistering sarcasm that had me belly laughing, and sometimes swerving on the road. Every so often he aimed his wit at me.

Mr. Grace was a man who pulled no punches.

Then it would usually get quiet until I asked him a few things. How did you get to work at such a cool place? How come Mr. Bernbach lets you come up with ideas and swim at the same time? And why do you complain about it so much?

He said to me, "You really have to love it."

"But you just told me the director was an idiot with no talent and your account guy was the worst you ever worked with and you've worked with a gorilla," I said confused.
He said, "That is love."

I never understood that until much later.

During those years going into the Doyle Dane Bernbach office, I met a lot of my father's peers and superiors and in some way or another not a single one would fit the notion of a typical businessman.

Today I am filled with gratitude for that old grey New York office building on Madison Avenue. It paved the way for a weirdo like me and so many others to have a profession where ideas mattered more than what you looked or acted like. You could work in the dark with your back to the world and create brilliance. Or rejoice in your ideas like an excited kid. Or better yet, get the job done by the side of a pool.

Men like Mr. Krone, Mr. Goldsmith, and Mr. Grace made it okay for all of us in every creative department to truly be oneself and feel comfortable on an *Island of Misfit Toys*.

Thanks fellas.

Do you know what we do here?

The first word Jay Chiat ever said to me was, "Terrible."

I was twenty-six years old and it was my first month at Chiat/Day when Mr. Chiat walked into my cubicle. He was dapper down to his shoe laces. He gazed at the tissues for the Macintosh II ad pinned up along the wall. He uttered "Terrible" over and over.
Finally he came upon my Hail Mary. A piece of paper so crumpled from being in and out of the trash it was almost unreadable. He crooked his head and smiled in that Jay-way I can only describe as both devious and genuinely proud.

The fourth word Jay Chiat ever said to me was, "Terrific."

Then he said, "Make it better" and walked out.

I wrote, rewrote and prayed that night for the ad to become better. However, there were some difficulties. I wasn't very good at the time and writing a perfect Apple headline is a tough thing for anyone to do.

Early the next morning I handed in a lackluster, expected, and non-Apple in every conceivable way, series of ads. And somehow it all landed on Fred Goldberg's desk. Mr. Goldberg was the President and Chief Executive Officer of the Chiat/Day San Francisco office.

Nervously awaiting the verdict on my ads, I tried to saunter unobserved past Mr. Goldberg's office as inconspicuously as Inspector Clouseau.

He was at his desk. Studying the ads. He saw me and raised those Spanish Inquisitor eyes above his reading glasses.

"You!" he said loudly.

Mr. Goldberg slowly rose from his chair bunching up my ads like toilet paper. By this time, heads were beginning to pop up from cubicles.

"These are not Apple headlines."

I stood there. Silent. My Pee-wee's Playhouse baseball cap was not playing well at the moment.

"Do you know what we do here?"

My face retained its Mt. Rushmore-ish expression.

"Do you want to know what we do here?"

Mr. Goldberg then started to point while speaking loudly, "Spend some time with him (Dave O'Hare), or in her office (he gestured to M.T. Rainey), or over there." (He gazed over to Mike Moser and Brian O'Neill's quarters).

He handed me the ads.

I realized suddenly for the first time I was at an agency that required me to work fast. Economically. Efficiently. On strategy. On target. On budget.

And now, I was also accountable for greatness?

Quickly I discovered *Good is the enemy of Great* was not just a slogan on a t-shirt around here.

One year later I walked into Mr. Goldberg's office with some ads for a new tech client in San Jose. This time I had written a hundred lines and with Brian O'Neill's help, whittled it down to eight. Mr. Goldberg held them up and quickly created two piles.

Great.

And crap.

Crap won but Great had three entries. And that was it. Mr. Goldberg dismissed me approvingly.

I lingered a few more moments than I should have, "Fred?"

Once again, the insinuating eyes over the reading glasses thing.

"Do you remember about a year ago you asked me do you know what we do here?"

Mr. Goldberg smiled and said, "Bring me back something better."

For the previous 365 days I had been watching and listening to the great talent in that office. The way they worked and believed in each other. It was a collective will to do what hasn't been done before. Or in simpler terms, it was a greed for greatness. And I wanted a piece of it.

I said to Mr. Goldberg, "Okay. No problem."

I was learning what must be done.

Make it terrific.

Then make it better.

Is the single essential selling point no longer essential?

Every rule in advertising can be broken.

Except one.

A single essential selling proposition.

Recently I took a look at the campaign for one of the largest auto manufacturers in the world. The single essential selling point on the website was "17% MSRP." The single essential selling point on social media was "highest loyalty rate of any car." The single essential selling point for outdoor was safety. And the TV communicated more like a multi-messaged disorderly direct mail piece than a commercial.

With the temptations of utilizing so many messaging platforms in so many different ways companies are now exposing customers to not one core truth, but an unruly mob of many truths.

An unwavering brand is not created with a scatter gun but a single bullet.

As a writer, it would be convenient to say this is not the fault of the creative department, but that is far from the truth. This is a group effort that requires guardian bulldogs in every step of the process.

This is the most exciting time in marketing history. We can explore endless creative executions. And still have a fully integrated message that is focused, relentless, and builds the story like pieces of a puzzle.

Plenty of brilliant marketers are out there doing just that. Delivering a multitude of messages on different levels that always goes back to the unique selling point. It's an incredible and inspiring thing to witness. And I am sure those marketers would tell us there are no easy answers.

But there is an easy solution.

Before you start any project, make sure it always comes back to that one thing.

It's essential.

Your most priceless asset is not on your resume.

One of the most valuable characteristics a creative adult can offer is the ability to think like a ten year old.

To approach complex problems with a sense of wonder, simplicity, unbridled fearlessness, and a complete disregard for normal. Of course all that naivety also has to be saddled with smarts, logic, and a deep sense of responsibility.

But make no mistake.

In most cases, the heart and magic of a great piece of communication comes from the Jr. in you, and not the Mr. or Ms.

There was a bottled water company from Sausalito, California called Watermark I was working on. They were a feisty group of investors who saw an opportunity in the growing bottled water market. They had very little money but wanted to make an impact.

One morning riding BART, I found an article buried deep inside The San Francisco Chronicle that amused me. In fact, the headline made me laugh out loud, *S.F.'s drinking water has wild pigs in it.*

It was 6 a.m.

Immediately my sophomoric and immature endorphins kicked in. I imagined a million dollar commercial for Watermark. It begins with wild pigs galloping freely in the Calaveras Reservoir. They're frolicking in slow motion. Like filthy wild stallions. Meanwhile, a couple is having a picnic in the tall green grass watching this debacle with fresh bottled water from Watermark. I think I might have even heard Pink Floyd's "Pigs" in there somewhere. Could one of our actors be wearing a Chief Wiggam t-shirt?

Who thinks like that at the crack of dawn?

A child in a sandbox.

I got to work and paraded the comical bit in the newspaper around. A frequent collaborator and great Art Director, Matt Smith's eyes blew up like a Warner Brother's cartoon character as soon as he saw it. Matt suggested a full page ad showing the article.

"You don't need anything else. Just the product and the logo," he said.

I suggested one line, *No Pigs*.

We giggled like school children.

The ad ran full page the very next day. Sales went up. Dramatically.

There are many years of experience on my resume but nowhere does it say that my most successful contributions occur when I think like a juvenile.

But I have learned you have to constantly feed that youngster with all the movies, music, literature and art you can digest.

You also have to protect it from an analytical and statistic-driven age so he or she doesn't dry up and wither away.

In short, you gotta love on that kid.

And it wouldn't hurt to put something on your resume like, "I can be an immense help to your business, company morale, and your clients because at heart, and sometimes in mind, I am just one big little boy."

Britney Spears, The Backstreet Boys, and the power of self-deprecation.

Self-deprecation is the ultimate people skill.

The art of truly opening yourself up to others and demonstrating the courage to occasionally look like a fool.

A prominent leader in the field of acquisitions says, "Self-deprecating humor is especially powerful. I use it whenever something goes dramatically wrong in a meeting. Typically, the glitch is a technological one that sidelines my entire pitch. Instead of sweating, freaking out, or clamming up, I chuckle and say, "When it comes to technology, our motto is 'Expect less.' And, as you can see, we deliver on that promise." It immediately defuses any tension in the room, displays my humanity, and gives us valuable time to fix the glitch."

It works in the movies as well as the boardroom.

Think George Clooney in *O' Brother, Where Art Thou?* or Lloyd Bridges in *Airplane*. Both films opened up entirely new career directions for the actors. The audience saw another more approachable side to a typically straight-faced commanding actor.

An old boss of mine once said if a candidate has a good sense of humor and doesn't think too highly of themselves, it's almost as important as a good portfolio.

He was right.

At the end of the day no one will ever take you seriously if you can't laugh at yourself.

One particular morning I walked into my office on Battery Street. Sun was out. No deadlines. Life was good. As I mounted the stairs and turned the corner to my office I noticed something peculiar.

My entire office was painted pink. Vibrantly pink. On the walls were stencils of hearts and unicorns. Posted up were too many Britney Spears, Backstreet Boys and N'Sync photographs to count. The desk was covered in fangirl paraphernalia. Heart shaped picture frames showcasing shirtless teens. There was even a diary that was actually handwritten with entries such as, "Ohhh I wish that J.C. would ask me out. He's so cool and sexy."

My private domain had become the bedroom of a girl named Amber who lived in the suburbs.

Within five minutes, everyone in the building heard about the gag in the Creative Director's office and wandered by with a wave or a guffaw. All I could do was laugh at myself.

Also on that particular day, my agency was being sold to prestigious ad giant Hill, Holliday, Connors, Cosmopulos Inc. It was a big event but I had forgotten about it due to the chicanery.

That is, until I looked down the hall and saw five distinguished men dressed in sharp conservative suits checking out their new acquisition. Soon they would walk by my work space. The office of a Creative Director who handled significant business with the agency.

Jack Connors, founder of Hill, Holliday, Connors, Cosmopulas, Inc. and legendary Boston adman passed my office first. The lauded and esteemed businessman looked at me with a sense of horror only reserved for the lepers of ancient Rome.
I sat there red-faced and mumbling incoherent remarks

showcasing world-class buffoonery as Bye Bye Bye played in the background.

That evening we all sat around at dinner and had a good laugh.

At my expense.

And I welcomed it, because the agency had a good outlet on a tense day. I also imagined it looked to our new owners that this was a strange, but fun place to work.

Best of all I think I earned some gold medals for bravery, trust, and humility from my coworkers and peers who orchestrated the shenanigans.

It's a proven fact that self-deprecation warms you up to others, brings people together as a team, unifies goals, and shows a level of maturity in leadership that many do not possess.

If you want a prime example, look at the White House.

Rough Meetings. Lunch with Billie Jean King and Bobby Riggs.

Once I had a snack with Billie Jean King and Bobby Riggs because my boss was too scared to be in between them. I was just out of high school and hired as a Production Assistant, this was my first job.

Fox Searchlight Pictures released a film called *Battle of The Sexes* starring Emma Stone as Billie Jean King and Steve Carrel as Bobby Riggs. In the trailer, it appears that both Ms. King and Mr. Riggs are having a little fun. That may have been true.

But on the day they were filming an Atari commercial at Astoria Studios in New York, I can most assuredly tell you this was not a harmonious couple. It was after the famous match and both athletes were making the rounds to cash in on some of the publicity they attained. Fair enough.

Just don't put a fresh-faced boy in the middle of it.

Which is exactly where I was. Frequently announcing the takes and snapping the clapperboard right in front of their faces. The scene was a simple one. Ms. King had just beaten Mr. Riggs at the Atari console and he looks at the camera and sheepishly says,

"She beat me again."

Trouble is, he was rushing and phoning it in. Even I could see that.

I have no idea what it must be like to be a celebrity and constantly doing commercials and press junkets. It must be exhausting.

And it probably brings out the real you very quickly.

Ms. King was a wonderful person. Gracious and smiling given her surroundings. 50 male crew members. 30 male Teamsters. The agency and Atari client. All male. Not another woman in sight. This probably was not her idea of a pleasant day.

Mr. Riggs was a caveman. Grumpy and rude. Ocassionally funny. Simple as that. Soon emotions behind that clapperboard were getting testy. Low disagreements between the stars became loud arguments.

"Get that thing out of my face!" Mr. Riggs said as I announced an umpteenth take.

A break was called and I was asked to bring the stars drinks, fruit, and cheese. My boss said, "You know, talk to them, make them feel comfortable." Again, I was about 17. I gathered a tray and walked up to the world famous competitors.

Having introduced myself earlier they smiled. Ms. King grabbed a juicy looking pear.

She asked me about me. If I played tennis. "How old are you?" (I had a baby face.)

We quickly got comfortable enough for me to joke about the Elton John song *Philadelphia Freedom* being written about her. I told her not enough Jimmy Page was in there.

There was only one pear.

"Get me a pear, just like that one," Mr. Riggs demanded.

Trouble is, there wasn't one.

I frantically loooked for a pear on the craft services table. I ran down the street to the market. No pears. Sweating and scared I ran back to Ms. King and Mr. Riggs.

"Where's my pear?" he snapped.

"I can't find one sir."

Ms. King said, "Take mine." It was half eaten. She probably enjoyed that.

"Jesus, I can't get a f@#%ing pear?"

My only defense was to make him feel exclusive. Like he was the only person in the room. I would go above and beyond for him. And I apologized with authentic humility.

I ran down the street and asked the grocer to get me his best selection of exotic fruits, fresh squeezed orange juice and a Snickers bar.

I brought them back on another tray and quasi-kneeled as I presented him with the goods. He now looked at Ms. King's measley pear and smiled triumphantly.

She smiled too. At me.

My first power play meeting.

And rudimentary as it was, ever since I have always felt like the two things you need to demonstrate at any meeting with a bully is to go above and beyond, and present authentic humility (toadying and brown-nosing are not the same thing).

I still believe that today, because there are a lot of people like Bobby Riggs out there.

As a side note, Mr. Riggs got what he wanted and we had a good time. The kind of attitude they convey in the trailer for *Battle of the Sexes*. A few laughs. Kind-hearted comments. Appreciation for one another.

He nailed the scene in three or four takes after break.

And off they went.

I thought to myself, now there goes a lady.

Years later I think to myself, God bless Billie Jean King for being courageous, brave and indestructible.

And carrying all that responsibility for women everywhere.

In a game where one person lost, and millions won.

Digital Killed the Copywriting Star.

Has the copywriter become a second class citizen of the digital age?

Once the web was a Beulah Land for copywriters to cultivate, create, and uniquely articulate brands of all sizes. It was beautiful. Paradise.

Now it is the verbal equivalent of a run down strip mall tended by shoddy writing skills, product managers with too many red pens and young talent that has obviously not been properly trained.

A little over a year ago I attended the yearly advertising and digital showcase for one of the largest, most prestigious companies on the planet. The 10,0000 square foot building that housed the festivities was covered with the most tasteful, beautiful, and arresting images, photography, and design one could ever see.

However, not a single inch of that building was devoted to celebrating good copy. There wasn't even a banner headline in sight.

And beyond the homepage of a typical site?

It gets worse.

The owner's manual in the glovebox of your car reads with more impact than the average website. Scary news, especially in a time when corporations should be treasuring meaningful messages to resonate in a consumer's psyche for years to come.
We should be keen to remember that writers are the only thing standing between the customer and conscious reasoning.

This voice must be heard and not shoehorned into a layout for design purposes.

Websites must look beautiful. And a striking image is worth a thousand words. But it's the writer who makes those words sing with impact, meaning and lasting value.

And let's not forget that great copywriters aren't born.

They are bred.

So, love on young writers. Give them the time and freedom to watch and learn from people who know how to write. And most importantly, hire people and portfolios based on good writing instead of good product knowledge. You can always learn the facts but you can't teach writing to a non-writer.

This is paramount in bringing back craft to a medium that has lost its vocal chords.

All hail the website with unforgettable design.

And long live the copywriter with the skill to give it life.

Growing up with one of the original Mad Men.

This is for my dad.

It's been said Don Draper was modeled closely after George Lois and Bob Levinson. I have no doubt that is true, especially since Mr. Levinson was a technical advisor on the show itself. And Mr. Lois had the charisma and looks of a Sean Connery stand-in. Mix that with their considerable talent and you can see why they were indeed Mad Men.

But I also choose to think of my dad as one of the original Mad Men. Like all of us he was not a perfect person, but his work for Volkswagen was.

The show was a brilliant recreation of Doyle Dane Bernbach in the 60's. I was there as a kid.

Like Don Draper himself, my dad was a hard drinking playboy who could command a room and deliver great work with the rest of them. (Honestly, I think they must have made booze weaker back then). I had seen these Doyle Dane Bernbach men drink a fifth of vodka, write a few spots, then go play tennis.

Before I go any further it must be acknowleged that my dad did all this great work with the aid of the brilliant Roy Grace, Bob Kuperman, John Caggiano, Len Sirowitz, Mr. Levinson, Bill Bernbach, and many other talented creatives, account executives and media folks.

He fathered three sons who are now in the advertising business. We are all pretty good but filling his shoes creatively is an almost impossible task.

He would rise at dawn and take the train into the city from Westport, Connecticut. He always took the 7:45 Stanford and Westport Express home. Back then, eating dinner with our father was a very rare thing. He worked hard. Mr. Bernbach did not appreciate half-baked ideas.

He was an extremely competitive man and that made him an exquisite salesman and probably propelled him to be the youngest Creative Director Doyle Dane Bernbach ever had at the time. I think he was 27. As an amusing aside, his competitiveness did not end on Madison Avenue. The man had my three brothers betting our allowances on darts, basketball, and badminton before we were teenagers. I have two natural brothers but my third brother in spirit, Scott Sheinberg, the General Manager of 22 Squared in Tampa Florida, would be over at my house almost everyday and Dad would take his money in 3-on-3 basketball or H.O.R.S.E. until Mr. Sheinberg grew to be six feet tall.

Commercials back then were spliced by hand. I remember sitting in unbearable boredom at Pelco Editorial. Mr. Pelco would cut and tape everytime there was a change and they would all look at the results through that little viewer. Dad and his partners were perched on stools looking over the editor's shoulder for days. Brutal. We are now very spoiled.

And the print ads. Oh, the print ads.

Dad would bring them all home mounted on foam core board and show them off. They were brilliant. And you can find many of them in the Museum of Modern Art. I think he expected us to hang them in our bedroom, and if I knew then what I know now, that would have been the case. But when I got a little older Pete Townsend was front and center on my wall.

I hope one day my father will be elected into the Advertising Hall of Fame. Very few writers, living or dead, possess such an immense body of influential work.

John Noble Sr. passed away at the age of 58 from an enlarged heart due to excessive drinking and chain-smoking. Like so many of his departed peers from the 60's, 70's and even the 80's, this lifestyle does take its toll. And it's a lesson to be learned.

In the end, Mad Men is about professionals who broke molds, sold campaigns with brilliant strategic thinking and changed the marketing world.

It's great television drama.

But my dad did it for real.

The Basics: Three tips for writing lines when stuck.

Tip number one.

Panic.

Yes, panic is good. Not the *I'm gonna get fired* panic. But the *I'm gonna make you weep, see God, and possibly even hug me as you read my lines* panic. This mixture of adrenaline, anger, and unrealistic thinking will propel you to come up with at least decent ideas. Sometimes even great ones. Fear is a writer's best friend. So embrace it. Use it. And chances are you won't have to show up to a meeting knowing there is better writing on cereal boxes than your MacBook.

Tip number two.

Use a thesaurus not for words, but ideas.

Sure it's the place to find a more consumer-friendly word than *verisimilitude*. However, I've also learned to view the thesaurus as the world's greatest headline writing assistant.

An example. Once while toiling on an airline account, I was assigned to write headlines promising "extraordinary service."

After a day of churning out empty marketing pablum I opened the thesaurus and looked up the word *service*. This gave me obvious synonyms like *courtesy* and *value*. A good place to start. Start writing lines with those words. But go further. Click on all the synonyms you find interesting. Then go to all the synonyms of those words. You'll find language like *overhaul, troubleshoot,* and *salvation.* Soon you'll have fifty relevant, clear and sometimes inspiring words that will spark other ways to look at your objective. After five minutes of searching I found the word *upright.* This conjured the plane-ism we've all heard, "Please adjust your tray to it's upright closed position." I thought if that line were humanized it could be interesting.

Please adjust your jaw to it's upright closed position.

Pair that line with a visual of a flight attendant doing something "extraordinary" and you have a decent thought with a little attitude. It made the client smile and buy the concept.

Thank you Mr. Roget.

Tip number three.

Create in darkness.

Pick up a pad and keep it on your chest when you turn out the lights at night. The mysterious and empty void of the dark are your most freeing hours of the day. You think differently. And when you get a line, a word, or a strategic vision, write them on your pad. Don't turn on the light. Major distraction. You'll get good at writing without seeing very quickly.

In the morning sometimes you'll wake up looking at the ravings of a loon. But more often you'll discover you've written a few gems you probably didn't have the stream of consciousness to write during the day.

Now, sit up and look at all the *nothing* on your computer.

Panic a little.

It'll do your headlines some good.

The M in GMO.

Back in the olden (or golden) days, GMO or Goldberg Moser O'Neill was one of the most successful independently owned advertising agencies in the country. It won big business. And a lion's share of top awards. The G, or Mr. Fred Goldberg was a hard driving, clever Chief Executive Officer who had the best eye for creative I have ever seen in an account man. The O, or Mr. Brian O'Neill was sharp, funny and had an uncanny ability to take a half-baked idea and turn it into gold.

The M, or Mr. Mike Moser, who tragically passed away on September 21, 2015, was my boss, my friend and one of the most ferociously talented art directors I have ever worked for and with.

With few exceptions, the creative greats in this business who have left us don't get their due. They get a paragraph in Adweek and that's about it. Mike deserved more. He gave more of himself to this business than just about anyone. To tell the truth, he was a stickler for detail and kind of a pain in the ass for absolute perfection. I can't tell you how many times I would present and re-present headlines to him with nothing but a single word change. But when all was said and done, you thanked him for it. It was better.

Mike was one of those rare agency owners that protected their employees. As an example: I was running a large account for a few years that had been terrorized and beaten senseless by an abusive client. So much so that many employees had to be consoled after meetings. One day after a large presentation to the international owners of this business, the derisive North American client switched gears in the middle of the meeting and after months of work, sold spots that were not agreed upon.

I asked the client for a face-to-face and summoned up every ounce of courage I had and let it fly. And so did the client. To say it was heated was an understatement. In fact, he pointed me to the door. In the back of the room Mike just watched and let me do my thing. He didn't step in and coddle the client, he knew this was needed. What I needed. And what my teams needed.

Afterward, the client was never rude to me again (a lesson for those who work for bullies - stand up to them). Mike stepped in after the fireworks and made sure each side was okay and we were. It was a management moment I shall never forget and one that is rarely seen today, at least I haven't witnessed it.

Mike was the keeper of the GMO brand. He lived advertising but didn't take it home. As good as he was, Mike was an ad man second. And a family man first.

This last little bit is not for the squeamish, but it does prove a point. It is without a doubt the greatest display of dedication to the craft of advertising as one will ever see.

We were assigned to create an emergency outdoor campaign for Bushmills. It was due in three days. On the day we were asked to do the project Mike had a scheduled vasectomy. Unfortunately it did not go well and there was an infection. He called me that night in great pain and said "Come over tomorrow and we'll work at the house." So I did. He was in severe pain but chose a clear mind over painkillers.

"What's the deal with the infection?" I asked.

He said "It will heal but my left one has swollen to the size of a tangerine."

I roared with laughter. He did the same. Next to his bed was a saucer but there was no tea cup. Mike suggested we go downstairs for lunch and work in a new environment. I found out what the saucer was for. He had to tenderly lay his "tangerine" on it while he walked. When I saw him do this under his robe, all I could do was roar with laughter again. And so did he. Again. Luckily, we stumbled on a good campaign. And I can tell you with great certainty that if I were in the same situation, no way would I have an art director over to my house to work on ads.

That was the kind of guy Mike was.

Passionate, assured and quite brilliant. I miss him dearly.

The 80/20 Theory.

Recently a popular business television program conducted an interview with two of the most powerful marketing executives on the planet. When asked about the current state of creativity one Chief Executive Officer concluded with this, "It used to be that 80% of every project depended on the creativity and strategic thought put into the crafting of a powerful messsage. 20% percent of that project's success relied on a smart and targeted media plan. Today those numbers have turned completely around and I don't see it going backward."

Being an advertising creative, I swallowed hard. According to two very well-informed gentlemen, 80% of a marketing campaign relies on science. And 20% on art.

Suddenly I longed for a boardroom that would ooh and ahh at a wall filled with creative ideas and strategic thoughts brought to life by an excited writer, art director and creative director.

Now all those "oohs" are for spreadsheets and "ahhs" are for visualization charts.

However, looking back objectively, it seems counting on the success of a project with 80% being dependant on the creative department was excessive and perhaps a little foolish.

And conversely counting on the success of a project with 80% designated to science today is also excessive and a little foolish.

From a creative standpoint, proof of this new equation surrounds us like air. Clear, meaningful, well-crafted, and striking ideas are an endangered species.

Of course, this 80/20 theory is not universal, but it's close.

Agencies are spending less on qualified creative personnel. Why? Because it doesn't take David Ogilvy to write a now acceptable banner headline that has very little meaning, wit, wisdom, selling power, and a tie-in to the big idea, if there is even a big idea at all.

Today this impressive scientific data is having the same effect on creativity as it did when we came face-to-face with something similar, yet less technical, almost fifty years ago.

It was called direct mail. And we all know how that turned out creatively.

By no means do I disparage this incredible technology and the amazing results than it generates.

But let's make it even better. Let's begin to once again emphasize the undeniable power of a brilliantly crafted message that ties into a tent pole idea and runs across all platforms.

Mathematically that would mean that we leave 60% of our plans to science.

And 40% back into art.

That means demanding great work and hiring outstanding creative people. Mentors. Rule breakers. And yes, experienced people like me who know a thing or two about getting noticed in even the most cluttered of places.

I can live with 40% devoted to art or creativity.

The issue then becomes who has the gumption to disrupt trends? Isn't that is what we are all paid to do?

Magicans don't reveal secrets. But good creative mentors do.

Advertising is not only an industry that eats its young, it doesn't feed them either.

I have never seen a time in this business when there are fewer mentors and teachers of great copy at marketing firms. Teachers are expensive and more than occasionally thought of as unnecessary. Just look at our school system.

Today young talent is hired and expected to create Olgivyian prose when about all they can do is write Wikipedia copy. So for those youngsters who have been hired by creative directors who promise you the world, but only deliver Toledo, here are a few tips.

Don't be Inspector Clouseau. Never sneak around looking at other writers work unless they are gracious enough to show it to you. Otherwise, two things will happen. You will probably write something derivative intentionally or, more likely, subconsciously. You are going to be a great writer because you are you. Find someone who truly cares and is willing to spend the time to help find your you. Or leave and go somewhere else.

Find a place that is patient and nurtures junior talent. That of course is easier said than done. Copy is hard. It takes years to master. And it takes a pro to teach you what to do and what not to do. Yes, there are slick talkers who can present the phone book and make it sound like Dickens. They never reveal their secrets. Because they don't have any.

The last thing a newbie needs is to be thrown under the bus. Most agencies are so under the gun with clients and overhead they will sacrifice your sanity and your soul without thinking twice. If you make it great, you get a pat on the back and a t-shirt. If you don't, you'll be shown the door pretty quick. Ask tough questions on your interview. Who will be your boss? What will you be working on? What are your responsibilites going to be? Is there someone to learn from? The average hirer couldn't care less about your career. It's really all up to you. And if you need money, take a crappy job until you find the right one. Just make sure you get out before you learn things you can't unlearn.

Don't be afraid to look like a fool. At one time or another every great creative person has been in your shoes and the ones worth a damn will respect you for being honest, humble and doing anything it takes to learn.

A considerable percentage of the people you are going to work with are inept. I'm not being cruel, it's just true. I can't tell you who they are but you will scope them out quickly. Treat them nice. In fact, treat everyone nice. Just don't listen to the buffoons. Pay good attention to something much smarter - your gut. Bottom line is for you to find people you can trust. Laugh with. Not be afraid to show ideas to. And respect, even when you disagree. Unless you are a born genius, listen.

Listen.

And then listen some more.

And CEO's, open your wallet and get your people some qualified training other than a monthly speaker. It makes fiscal sense. Because once your new hire gets to be great, it'll be the best kept secret you have.

Mentally overcoming that trip back to the drawing board.

"Go back to the drawing board" are the six most devastating words one can hear in business other than, "You look good for your age."

If you carefully study the dynamics of your situation, you can overcome. There's a lot more to it though, than just going back and hitting the books.

Pyschology plays a larger part here than business acumen. I have been subjected to the brutality of "your ideas are mediocre" more times than I can count.

Believe me, I know the pain.

Like the five stages of death, there are four stages of advertising death after walking out of your boss's door humming, "I'm a loser baby, so why don't you kill me." Without trying to sound like Plato, these stages will allow you to become stronger the more times you face this situation, and you will face it alot.

First is **anger**. *Everyone else is wrong, you are right. One day I will own an agency. And they will clean my toilets.*

Then comes the delusion **I am not cut out for this**. *I love dogs, I can clean animal cages for a living at the dog shelter and be happy.*

Followed by **displaced positive anger**. *I will come back with something so good that my boss's boss will see I am better than him or her and get them fired.*

Finally, you get to a place where you reach **acceptance** and *you are going to beat this and prove to yourself, and the world, that you are one of the best in this business.*

For a seasoned vet this usually all takes place in the span of about five minutes. If you are new, it could last a day or longer. So go back to your boss with questions, **and this is really important here**, go back with some solutions. Ask him or her specifically what went wrong? What if we did this? What if we did that?

Don't forget your boss has about five **"go back to the drawing boards"** him or herself everyday. Their creative advice might have been cryptic or hurried, but give them a break and solve some things on your own.

No one likes to tell someone to go back to the drawing board. It's unpleasant for you. And means your CD probably feels under the gun. Or worse, he or she has to solve it themself.

Never, ever let it get that far.

You can beat this with a little psychology, motivation and a strong belief in yourself.

And let's not forget the fact that when you go back to the drawing board, 99.9% of the time **you always create a better idea.**

The best six words in the business.

What do you tell a creative person when you couldn't sell the work?

#1 Never wait for more than a half hour to call your team(s) and let them know how a meeting went. They are not babies but they have probably spent a good amount of time working to make you look good. I have worked under a few CD's that walked in the next morning, mumble about a failed meeting, and shut the door. If the meeting was a roaring success, I bet you'd get that call within thirty minutes the preceding evening. It's a hard, hard thing to tell those people their efforts have gone not unappreciated, but not appreciated enough for a green light. That usually indicates a healthy lack of cojones.

If everyone is okay without a call, then your team doesn't care.

Apathy is a dangerous thing.

I remember when I had a campaign in the running, I would try to behave somewhat nonchalant. If a meeting ended at three-thirty and I didn't get a call, there was usually one reason. The idea didn't sell.

#2 If you're a good CD who nurtures their department, what do you say to these poor souls who just gave a big chunk of their lives to make you look good? Tell them how great the work was and mean it. Quote lines. Playback reactions from certain visual scenes. If you can do that with vim and vigor, you've proven you know the work. And if you can't do that, it's obvious you put very little into selling the idea. Young creatives may be naive but they can smell a song-and-dance person a mile away.

#3 Don't be a song-and-dance person. Those are the types that talk pretty. But can't write pretty or can't visualize pretty. Everyone loves a showman except the people that usually pay the price for his or her glory - the teams. Turn off the spotlights and get in a room with your teams and hammer out a strategy that focuses soley on the issues at hand. There is nothing worse than getting those three dreaded words, "Do something different." Lead by example.

#4 Don't blame the failure of a sale on a client. Most clients are smart. And they don't think like we do. They could have had a bad day. They could have had a bomb dropped on them fifteen minutes before the meeting. I've never had a client I could fully blame for the outcome of a crappy meeting (except one), and everyone I worked with in San Francisco knows that to be true. So look in the eyes of your copywriters, designers, UX team, art directors, producers, creative assistants, comp artists, photographers, media specialists, and planners and tell them the truth. They can handle it.

Breaking the news without breaking morale is a learned skill. Which makes #5 the most important departmental rule of all:

Respect.

Meet the new open office. Same as the old open office.

Great creative rarely emerged from 1955, and it's not much different in 2018.

Planning, developing UX, design, and managing accounts are positions I am not qualified to comment on. But I do know about writing words and content with an occasional good visual to boot.

Creativity is not dissimilar to sex. It takes at least two people. A private room. Some experimentation. Finally, a moment of ecstacy.

The concept of the open office/no doors policy was ironically reimagined by one of the greatest creative minds in advertising history during the 90's. And I am pretty sure this is not what Mr. Chiat had in mind when he thought of it.

Creation feeds on peace, focus, quiet, and no one shouting,"Who will come back from the ashes in Infinity Wars?"

Greatness has always come from solitude. From Plato to Jackson Pollock to Walt Disney.

The open office is a Brave New World. Loud, noisy and unproductive.

Let's be frank, putting everyone in one space is not a new way to work. Or a vocational experiment. It's a cost cutting measure for upper management to provide board members a nice boardroom.

And I am not only talking about the giants. Small agencies have adopted this open office scenerio as well.

The open office may be a brilliant idea for folks in the parts of our business that don't require creativity. There certainly is a cross-pollination effect. There are fewer phone calls. And people from diffferent disciplines can communicate face-to-face.

That may be a genius of a concept. Don't know.

Not everyone has to have a fancy oak work space but there must be a smarter solution for serious concepting than ten small think-tank rooms that are usually used for teleconferencing.

I'd be a fool to say I knew the answer.

Besides, it would be too difficult at this moment. I wrote most of this in a Barnes and Noble where there were too many tables and too much noise.